Coloring Book

Maggie Swanson

DOVER PUBLICATIONS, INC.
Mineola, New York

This whimsical collection features fantastic flower designs with adorable woodland creatures frolicking throughout. There are thirty different scenes and a bonus page for you to draw your own flowers. The detailed pictures are great fun for the enthusiastic colorist, and displaying your work is easy because the pages are perforated for easy removal!

Bibliographical Note

Flower Fun Coloring Book, first published by Dover Publications, Inc., in 2016, contains all sixteen images from Dover's *Floral Fantasies Stained Glass Coloring Book* (2013) and fourteen new illustrations, all be Maggie Swanson.

International Standard Book Number

ISBN-13: 978-0-486-80215-2
ISBN-10: 0-486-80215-9

Manufactured in the United States by RR Donnelley
80215901 2016
www.doverpublications.com

Draw Your Own Flower Design